Inside Song is what Jean Toomer might have written if he lived long enough to be alive "today," after, say, 1964, 2009, Michael Brown, after—in brief—impossibility, a cognate—not antonym—of "liberation." Titled with sass ("This poem is called Zora Neale Hurston because."), directed by a historical consciousness nimble enough to glide among the iterations of what Amiri Baraka once called the blues impulse (from jazz to r&b and "after") and confounding master and slave narratives of evolution or decline, *Inside Song* orients itself toward the horizon that is black music, that prospect of, and model for, a freedom which beckons and warns: "Study the bee. Study the baited bird."

Tyrone Williams, author of *As iZ*
and judge of the Omnidawn Poetry Chapbook Prize

Steve Dickison's *Inside Song* will remind you that music is the fundament of poetry and poetry is music and one of the ways our wounds can be healed and we can sustain those around us is through sound. These poems attempt to do this work by being attuned to the "inside song" "cultivated somewhere beyond the horizon line." Dickison's ears are open and his poems bear the mark of listening to a common bell. But in the surveillance state it is not only poets who listen and make songs, so the book ponders how we form renegade songs and build passage to what we have to do without knowing in advance what that is. Because, as the book says, what befalls us befalls us together. Rolling around in the cinders and phoenixing therefrom. Palpating the signs, raising the names, and listening always listening.

Alli Warren, author of *I Love It Though*

Inside Song

PREVIOUS BOOKS

DISPOSED (THE POST-APOLLO PRESS, 2007)

Inside Song

Steve Dickison

OMNIDAWN PUBLISHING
OAKLAND, CALIFORNIA
2018

Cover art:
Feet Don't Frail Me Now, from *Wetlands Journal*, 2001–Present
by Julie Ezelle Patton

Cover typeface: Kabel LT Std
Interior typeface: Kabel LT Std, Cronos Pro

Cover design by Trisha Peck
Interior design by Cassandra Smith

Offset printed in the United States
by Thomson-Shore, Dexter, Michigan
On 55# Glatfelter B18 Antique
Acid Free Archival Quality Recycled Paper

Library of Congress Cataloging-in-Publication Data

Names: Dickison, Steve, author.
Title: Inside Song / Steve Dickison.
Description: Oakland, California : Omnidawn Publishing, [2018]
Identifiers: LCCN 2018015799 | ISBN 9781632430625 (pbk. : alk. paper)
Classification: LCC PS3604.I298 A6 2018 | DDC 811/.6--dc23
LC record available at https://lccn.loc.gov/2018015799

Published by Omnidawn Publishing, Oakland, California
www.omnidawn.com   (510) 237-5472   (800) 792-4957
10 9 8 7 6 5 4 3 2 1
ISBN: 978-1-63243-062-5

Contents

Zora Neale Hurston
10 Poems and a Legend

◆ ◆

"Anything you do we put you in sing"

ZNH

1. "I could have never got out of the Police Orchestra"

Gétatchèw Mèkuria

War-songs also are a part of the repertory, war-chants, one they like to do they call this "chase after them and beat them down," so you understand what's coming at you when this particular music raises up its head, it's not without agency that the players the way they're arranged in the mathematics of this equation need to stay inviolate, unmessed with, thus not to be turned into so many items of luggage getting opened up and rifled thru, given they are travelers on the planet, have been so, even with a healthy preference for the orchestra to maintain a steady focus, stationed at home in Harar.

2.

The arrangement, for pep band, of farangis, on farangi instrumentation and staging, costume, delivery system, way heavy manners of stumbling-block drafted to serve the sounds, some big custodial sweepers-up told every little star in its passway how it better watch itself, watch itself watching itself, otherwise all stars get set upon by set-uponners, only listen, lead with your ear, it's the lesson these farangis, these foreigners calling his-and-herself the Ex band, make their way, each one of them, "whether s/he has made it up or s/he is only dreaming it," otherwise how did they learn to play Ethiopian.

3. "the word changes / the moment / i write / it"

William Rowe

Driven into a part of the city had only been gone past before, industrial in earlier before-time spelling vacant at present, opportunists see brightness although the skies fail to part, sun leaked thru cloud covers, lambswool undyed yellow-brown beam pouring over dampness, the day is still day out, out in it one parks the car stepping into attempted carnival subculture of costumed features, are they animating particles of speech, a vapor or sensation, sub-electric, felt being passed among practitioners as can be found to be given off by clusters of large plants, say, sequoias.

4. "what we're trying to destroy is a method too"

Masabumi Kikuchi

You come away with the sensation that the dream's encased in gelatin, not the translucent-walled bead or bean vitamin supplements arrive in, but the soft flexible jellyfish texture, around the dream this floating nebular substance outside of which, it's like what is outside the universe, it appears to me, that place, over there, to be noplace at all, still inside the dream you need to play the instrument, pray then how are you supposed to do this if you don't have on the silver jacket, *argento*, the inmate/contestant next to you is wearing his, riveted to his charts mapped out in front of him, the inside passage to the inside song.

5. "it's been very devastating this craving for meaning"

Avital Ronell

Look at those dogs over there playing, distracted plenty by the hypersweet pitch of their waitperson's performance-based labors, a lost hour inserting itself between witnessing these tectonic plates of foodstuffs arriving and the first fork of it touching tongue and teeth, undecipherable nuggets, how often greater than the human mouth encompassing them, cultivated somewhere beyond the horizon-line, *he remembers there were gardens* "in this absolute contingency of being," with his right paw he'd begun conducting the cadences of speech, she'd had put on her the necklace of babyfist-sized amber tears.

6. "Streaky cloudy at the top of the sky"

Jess, <u>Narkissos</u>

Kathryn with a K, KATÁ-, uncountable WAVES BREAKING ON ROCKS, hearing as many swells of voice and fallings away as there are elements of force, underpainted by dream as MATA-, MATAR, cf. *matador*, lit. killer, with its accompanist/its accomplice, clear-eyed or "white-eyed," slender arms prominently featured onstage as performers themselves to be braided in knots, "to go" and "to go around" shoulders and waists, the way one says "I'd like that *to go*, please, around me," what's intrinsic to her actions as to her name is that there's no one who wouldn't like that to be done to them, the full sequence, channeled by gravity to run across property lines, a very dear advertisement.

7. "I thought you had doubts of my additional powers"

Joëlle Dussuyer

Thus, Ferdinand Jellyroll Morton 1938 May into June with Alan Lomax, the tune rec. 1939 is a favorite identified with notoriously undocumented worker cornet titan Charles Buddy Bolden, conveyed up the river a ghost of himself, sealed silent, June 1907 to known death Nov. 4 1931, stationed JACKSON ASYLUM, viz Jelly Lord floating the lyric ventriloquizing BB, thinking he heard Bolden shout // let that bad air / that foul air out, with your Funky Butt played and sung to be recorded two occasions, slow drag with a lurch heading, gentleman Sidney Bechet sopranimics, small-barreled cluster band into the release at 0.00 seconds remaining, thrown against the wall to an adjoining apartment.

8. "there's a good echo in the projects, until people yell at you to shut up"

David Henderson

They'll dock your pay, they'll get rough with you, then they'll blame it on us, they said, is how it came to me, it has its ways, I sit with them to take in how they do it, so until I manage to fail well enough to where they agree I've done so, the virtue of this medium is this, it can come back around wearing its appearance/its apparition suitably different, differ-ent-LEE, thank you, I am given to understand that the management's message is *this has always been the* VISION, cemented between twin jawbone pliers, we love you, You the Beautiful, but and so here's a program of uplift and improvement to get right with, get right with this.

9.

Where were we, we were out in the field, the animal and I, doing fieldwork, done with the wind beating down on its drumhead, corona of hill dusted with red facepowder, the yellows diluted by addition of neutral base pigment, noise isn't noisy it's ash of sonic integers, the players set it out for incineration on the curb in buckets, scattered to the corners, in fieldwork it's requisite that there be at minimum greater than the one of yourself, the interlocutor, to toss around the ball of wax, so after the balltoss there is for the record a second set of digits to palpate the raw inscriptions engraved on the moonstone, its cheesy soft surface, to interpret these signs you have to get into the grave.

10. "You Thought You Could Build a World Without Us"

Sun Ra, The Antique Blacks

Child actors vested with burden or task of performing the person as agent of the act of walking up and down in the earth, to be advocates of transparency, how come, as if we're ourselves see-thru as this thin piecemeal rain that happens around here touches down on the deck of the mothership more like a veil than percussion, Mister Milford Graves he is a healer, un curandero, tells me once it gets adequately molested my heartbeat can be arranged to be distributed amongst the general population as a salve against THE WORLD writ large, floodlit, as if to shovel daylight off the deep end.

T H E   L E G E N D

goes like this. The rumored Buddy Bolden Cylinder, stuff of fable, re-broke the surface late last evening. Not the sounds to be sure yet the rumor that it, the Cylinder, could exist, the ring of his horn laid into the bell of the recording angel's horn before he became becalmed, one of the disappeared. ◆◆ This poem is called Zora Neale Hurston because. It was done that way on purpose. She had been, again, mishandled by her keepers. She was left out in the sun. The sun btw has been lovely, buffed white matte finish, filtered by cloudload of mist off the Western Ocean to our backs, a breeze thru the cloud camisa to rub off the edge, threatening early summer. ◆◆ One night like this night, up late at the machine and leaning into the soundspace chez Lomax, "the man who recorded the world," I was entertained by Mr Jelly Lord. Men are funny, they can be. Talk about alone together. I've forgotten more than anyone'll ever know about my Herculean staying power. Why don't you shovel on a little more coconut oil? I've come to like my peas without the rice, my rice without the white jackets painted on. With the white scraped off. Like Bobby 'Blue' Bland. ◆◆ Jelly, that is to say if you're feeling West African, Djeli, spoke on in his manner, Lomax supplying perforations in his. To my recollection Morton nudged by Lomax called up Buddy Bolden and the legend of the Funky Butt. It may have been otherwise than how I remember it. What sort of being talks this way? ◆◆ Morton asserts what he asserts, Lomax wants to pad some flesh onto the Misty School skeleton labeled Buddy Bolden. Funky Butt the song renominated "Buddy Bolden's Blues" comes our direction credited Bolden and Morton. Fair enough, the founding mist and the composer-arranger who would be founder, fonder. Jelly Roll graces BB's signature song with strokes of instrumentation as with his voice, the call, shaking back thru the scrim. When in a further iteration Nina Simone in her way plucks up the thread out of Ellington and after Joya Sherrill, Bolden on the other side sits in both for Joshua at Jericho on ram's horn, plus, Black Jesus calling his flocks from across the river. He's calling his flocks now. What do they call it again when the person gets pictured in the mirror of songs as People of the Book that got printed in we-the-people-who-are-darker-than-blue ink? ◆◆ Somebody by happenstance on my birthday in 2009 posted a mess up on the World Wide Web and titled it *The Best of Zora Neale Hurston*. The Florida Memory Project needs to be consulted in order to unconceal titles for the tracks given odd half-typed identifiers here in lieu of anything like proper names (Bella, Crow, Dat Old, Ever, Shove, Tilly, Wake, etc.). Even María Sabina got the Smithsonian treatment. What is here are songs, 18 pieces for solo voice recorded, most of them, June 18 1939 in Jacksonville, Florida. She is singing. I get excited when she does that. You would too. ◆◆ For example, she speaks as preamble: "This is a song called Tampa / I've known it ever since I could remember / so I don't know who taught it to me / but I heard it sung in my native village when I was a child / not in front of the old folks of course [she sings] 'Thought I heard somebody say / your nasty butt, your stinky butt, take it away (x2) / I do not want it in here'" ◆ ◆ Everybody in the country knows, it's a skip-rope song, the Funky Butt. In the second verse, it goes: 'O I'm so glad that the lawyers passed / the women in Tampa got to wash their ass (x2) / O I do not want it in here.' An editor transcribing the lyric for W.W. Norton in 1999 renders these two lines: 'Oh I am so glad that the lawyers pay / The women in Tampa got to watch the air' ◆ ◆ I met her on the corner of 1983 and San Pablo Ave. Cold June sun lighting up the dayglo insulated parkas on the neighborhood kids doing the passeggiata, slower than you want to know. If you were watching the air when that song went by, could you recognize Buddy Bolden's number marching in? Kids know, and are known to love the Funky Butt. Click *here* if you find parfum de cul arresting. ◆ ◆ At the family's instigation, near forty years after the deluge, Pablo Neruda's corpse is to undergo toxicology testing. For poisons. Neruda. Was it the same year as Jorge Ben asked, how to put it? *Errare humanum est.* Human is a mistake, and then what? In the meantime the Munchkins have dug up from its grave "Ding Dong the Witch is Dead" and are chanting the song in stadia and street. Ringing home the dead. Viva the Munchkins. As Andrew Hill told me this morning, he never got much work, but he always managed to keep a little office going out of which he might *get work*. ◆ ◆ You think that's funny? You're pretty jolly. A jolly depressive, that's a diagnostic rubric in the DSM-VI. Jolly? Jelly. That book doesn't exist, does it? See what I mean?

---

iv13

Liberation Music Orchestra

1.

"He had a special cymbal (I guess all of them have their special
cymbal) that sounded like a waterfall, just like Kenny Clarke on
'Swedish Schnapps' with Bird. Billy could bring people into his
time, a time that enveloped you."

Charlie Haden on Billy Higgins

The "Portrait of Robert Thompson (as a young man)" that band
gone drafted into the LMO, under the premise / that there /
there is such a thing as liberation and as liberation music.
"You could be further under" erstwhile daylight,
how the clouds / seem to be not moving at the same time wind
the lime tree registering applause, draft of it.
Waft of it "out there" and "inner ear" chained to yonder wall.

Even the true mirror / reversing the reversal
of the mirror per se, doesn't say ME back to me. "HOW / MANY /
ENEMIES / MAKE / A / SOUL" has to be placed under "science"
under "fiction" to not be invisible ink. Mr Henderson was drafted
into Mr Coleman's organization 10 September 1971, to tear down
in order to tear down   the belief that my mirror
says ME back to me. "You could be further under," the day
has to start again / if it wants to be half splendid as the night.

Take / eat. This salad / given for me. This do the do
in living memory of the living. "DON'T / RACE / MY / FACE"
David Henderson is in the science-fiction room they pitched,
if it's time-bound who told them that, workers at "the transcon-
figuration" (Nahum Chandler) "of the limits of existence in
our time" will come, nobody let them build this / exactly nobody.
Julius Hemphill and Dewey Redman were cousins, out of Texas,
and they were all cousins of Ornette / So said Mr Ehrlich.

The room, could it know / what was happening to it
it jumps up from its chair, sits back down again / out of not-
knowing, anepistēmē coming down, rain on the roof, like that.

Like note/s preceding a downbeat, floating elevator pre-tapshoe
sounded not hammered home, "You could be further under"
That world you were inside of / so familiar you'd think it was
a proper place / to lay one's head. Said, w/ ready enthusiasm,
with the generosity of someone pleased at being impossible /
at being impossibly asked to be pleased. In the what-falls-down,
what befalls one by the rule of will-befall-somebody-else.

Who "I" is, talks like that you want to / how it makes you / How you say in a day I might read a paragraph, might maybe listen while its sonics undergo the way they do the things they are being bent on. House of Between, House of will-not-be-plowed-down / plowed-over, given for you. This do the do.

Where the door gets painted shut you leave half the door exactly
like that, half painted closed so it's an observation work of half-here.
Not in remembrance, in full possession of half-here, painted closed so
as if nothing to be seen here. / Some hyperplatonic ideal, capsized
its cargo invisibly shattered by the impact with the flying subtraction
mechanism / grind your garden to salt to prove you can't do the do.

Sometimes I sit on the Ocean, sometimes I sit under the ground. A parenthesis half closing me round. Sometimes time goes boom boom boom. / In folk time. / The listener or reader could've slept in the hole that yawned open it was so. / These explosions watermarks on the photos / clouds after explosions / as if they're property / They're proper. / Belong to someone and someone will want them.

These explosions that have / under them / people, little persons, heat
dumped on summer camps where the median child-person / is who.
Liberation music would address the envelope the violators fail
to recall could be opened by themselves / Who be so previously
occupied "controlling the narrative" (for one) even the envelope /
opaquing out the inside song / is out of reach. Sandy beach.

What was that world "like" you just came
back from? / Tell it everywhere, you go as if 1964 they allowed
Staples family band, they don't / line a hymn, these people raise
a hymn at Newport. These explosions. "You could be further
under" effects of the shelling on those not themselves being shelled /
being sheltered / "Tears jumped up in my eyes" / Where she sang.

Summer 1964 the Staples family singers raised liberation songs
at Newport. / Only with the discontinuous. / Liberation music wants
to get up and moan about it, line the track to raise the hem /
The hymn of "the world" when it's exhausted, when it lays down in the
cinders rolls around in it / Ashen voiced or ashen / bodied the di-
amond faced kids versus the plume of smoke out of the skyways.

Turn your airport down. / Raptor oughtn't to be tied
to that wall of sound / rushing at their faces. The birds not to be
blamed nor tarred. Staples stapled the song to the cloud. Down in
1964. Liberation music how it starts out rumbling, then gets to be
a thing, and the handclapping build up, and the whole song keep un-
folding / And nobody's left out of what the sound undoes. / What it say
to fold you in / its heft and woof its / crowd-voice massed choir
vox "You could be further under" its typewriter platen its / typology.

———————

July 2014

2.

"I'm intrigued by sleep — I keep a log of nightmares."

Ran Blake

The way they say it is they say 'melody lover,' he played that freaky
shit but he swung back into boom boom boom / into folk time /
he'd vacation there though he wouldn't go over to the freak-side.
His burden / lay in the shade / of the lone palmtree terror from the air
neglected to collapse in the marbled grey monochrome, the grey on
poisoned wheatfield monolandschaft. / Stir the palette w/ a cereal
spoon / the bowl of crushed vernacular. Skydust. From-the-sky-dust.

"I" was carrying you around in a little basket. Apple image in the eye of the bearer-across. We'd lay down in the landschaft burrow a core sample into the / cereal bowl of new ruin, new bedlam. Like a cat with a dog's bone. Until indifferent. We didn't think we were / we were playing in the voice-bowl / the dog ran away w/ the spoon to ladle from-the-voice-dust. Melopoeia poured across the marbled paper land-schaft. If a half / if a half-ton / if a half-ton bomb don't break mother's back.

"Can you paint this?" voice-paint thought to ask / seeing the all but the palmtree plowed over. Century old picture we ought to be shamed at having to see / having to lift psalms over. Like a grape / waiting to be trod song. Footfalls on the ceiling you hear out the window in the video / Punched-in perforations in the piano-roll w/ perforations yet to be punched in. / Sound not so silent. Are-there-bird voices / are-there-tree-for-bird voices. Study the bee. Study the baited bird.

"Point from which creation begins" in St. Louis. Oliver
Lake fallen under the bindu. Mr Haden in the tropics downriver
entertaining radiowave watchers from the kinderposition. Young
Mr Lake upriver putting it into the / common bell of the horn. "Was
it a plastic instrument?" / The icecream maker the / storer of medicines
for nightmares. / Horse who didn't know the way to pull the desert sledge.

"They delivered all the wind right here." There ain't no redlight burning, greenlight keep being handfed directly to the violators. Liberation music revisions scenes inside the act inside the playhouse burning down. The teahouse / the waterhouse / the firehouse, that's the waterhouse re-spelled for the spelling-challenged. Grandmother's house the slice-of-piehouse. This unnamed young woman in voice-of-the-voice-where-she-sanghouse / Does nobody know her name / nobody raised her name.

Did it matter the song's words get buried in the song. Ferguson. / around the corner from where waits / at the ready at / The drop of the hammer on the ring-like-a-bellway. When we're melted down and forged into a handbell / What can be rung by the nobody / the no-fly is strapped down over / Said "to provide safe enclosure" to the violators gifted second-hand armadas for domestic operations on the level of the neighborhood. The level off.

"You could be further under" liberation music's orchestration
like a waterfall. Some call it firefall / falls from the air you'd
breathe by the fact you're there. / In this time not separated
in time / "could bring people in," Mr Haden said of Mr Higgins,
his time. "We were all feeling the same way" in L.A. That
the prospect was and is and it remains emancipatory /

At every "measure" / at every proportion. The lion feedtime /
the lamb lie down on the corner no intention on their mind time
"could bring people in" / Could make an envelope to roll around in-
side its time. Turquoise t-shirted man walks into a barrage.
Not even of no good / Of no good like what's left after they vacuum
the lounge after the party people went. / That void, of whatever / ask
Who suits up dressed to kill to keep convenience stores in operation.

Whereas: "We read the text from left to right / right to left, / tear
the whole text down / reinvent it every possible way that we can imagine
Drop out parts of the text / never Add anything to the text / but com-
pletely destroy the text / reinvent the text over and over, leave out
parts of the text. / Then we know something about / what we're about to do."
Henry Threadgill's at the Library of Congress (26 October 2013) / Take
the card catalog home with you, they don't use that thing anymore.

"Those Who Eat Cookies" know. / Unsettled, the not-to-be-settled. Nobody's buying that the nightmare's the kind where we / don't wake up from it. Exactly nobody. Neither that it's driving nobody's 'archaic mother' around on its ride / to downtown and home again / it's not that kind of animal / Our collective who-can-sleep drummed up and handfitted a saddle to its spine to slide down Fl-orrisant. / And dig the two drummers on "You Know The Number."

"Here we touch on oneself" it reads / the sign over the portal enter-
ing into how to do / what isn't known in any advance of to have
to do. In order to touch on oneself, "you could be further under"
Liberation music's completely-destroy-the-text telephone call to
disorder the wrong order put in place before we got to where we /
were staying. Where if we lived / we would be by now. Liberation music
writes over top the words and phrases / sentences you've previously written.

How "being exposed to the people making the music" (Charlie Haden to Bari Scott) changes everything. Autumn leaves, summer circles halfback around with evident hole in its rib / cage to its front-end / loaded crown of the head / Where the cloud / where the crowd collected. Night and Day. Michael Brown. Rhymes w/ brown study. Kind of cloud little moonlight bounces down off it, umbral.

_____

Aug/Sept 2014

Notes

The title *Inside Song*—my gratitude to C.S. Giscombe for finding it (hearing it) in the poems—is after William Parker's extended project, The Inside Songs of Curtis Mayfield. "Every song written or improvised has an inside song which lives in the shadows, in-between the sounds and silences and behind the words, pulsating, waiting to be reborn as a new song" (WP, liner notes to *I Plan To Stay A Believer: The Inside Songs of Curtis Mayfield*, AUM Fidelity, 2010).

Zora Neale Hurston's "Tampa," the lyric to which is quoted, is among her WPA/Federal Writers' Project recordings, 1935–39, accessible online at the Library of Congress American Folklife Center, and at the Florida Memory Project. The song, with her other recordings, is transcribed in Pamela Bordelon's *Go Gator and Muddy the Water: Writings by Zora Neale Hurston from the Federal Writers Project*, W. W. Norton, 1999.

Charlie Haden, Liberation Music Orchestra founder, leader, composer and contrabassist, is quoted from a radio interview conducted by Bari Scott, recorded June 8, 1985, at KPFA-FM, Berkeley, that was rebroadcast by Art Sato (his sister having found a cassette recording she'd made from the original broadcast) on his Saturday KPFA program "In Your Ear," shortly after Haden passed, July 11, 2014.

Further sources at:
https://www.omnidawn.com/sources-inside-song/

Thanks to those who kindly published these works, at times in earlier versions: *Amerarcana* (ed. Nicholas Whittington); *Transfer* (ed. Jessica Marasco); *BAX 2015: Best American Experimental Writing* (eds. Douglas Kearney, Seth Abramson, Jesse Damiani, Wesleyan UP, 2015); and *Pallaksch. Pallaksch.* (eds. Elizabeth Robinson, Steven Seidenberg).

Steve Dickison is author of *Disposed* (The Post-Apollo Press, 2007). Director of The Poetry Center at San Francisco State University, he teaches at that school and at California College of the Arts, and lives in San Francisco.

INSIDE SONG
by Steve Dickison

Cover art:
Feet Don't Frail Me Now, from *Wetlands Journal*, 2001–Present
by Julie Ezelle Patton

Cover typeface: Kabel LT Std
Interior typeface: Kabel LT Std, Cronos Pro

Cover design by Trisha Peck
Interior design by Cassandra Smith

Offset printed in the United States
by Thomson-Shore, Dexter, Michigan
On 55# Glatfelter B18 Antique
Acid Free Archival Quality Recycled Paper

Publication of this book was made possible in part by gifts from:
Mary Mackey
Francesca Bell
Katherine & John Gravendyk, in honor of Hillary Gravendyk
The Clorox Company
The New Place Fund

Omnidawn Publishing
Oakland, California
Staff and Volunteers, Fall 2018

Rusty Morrison & Ken Keegan, senior editors & co-publishers
Gillian Olivia Blythe Hamel, senior poetry editor & editor, *OmniVerse*
Trisha Peck, managing editor & program director
Cassandra Smith, poetry editor & book designer
Sharon Zetter, poetry editor, book designer & development officer
Liza Flum, poetry editor
Avren Keating, poetry editor & fiction editor
Anna Morrison, marketing assistant
Juliana Paslay, fiction editor
Gail Aronson, fiction editor
SD Sumner, copyeditor
Emily Alexander, marketing assistant
Terry A. Taplin, marketing assistant
Matthew Bowie, marketing assistant
Mia Raquel, marketing assistant